Christmas 1979
Best wishes Richard
As always!
L. xo

# Horses

David Street

## A Working Tradition

McGraw-Hill Ryerson Limited

Toronto Montreal Halifax Vancouver New York London
Sydney Mexico Panama Johannesburg Düsseldorf
New Delhi Kuala Lumpur Auckland São Paulo

# Contents

Horses: A Working Tradition
Copyright © McGraw-Hill
Ryerson Limited, 1976.

Design by Newton & Frank

Printed and bound in Canada

Canadian Cataloguing in Publication Da

Street, David, 1947-
  Horses

ISBN 0-07-082283-2

1. Horses — Pictorial works.   I. Title.

SF303.S77    636.1    C76-017152-1

# Preface

This book is really just a portrait, a composite of photographs and words, depicting an outmoded way of life in which horses played a vital role. A few generations ago the horse was a power source to be reckoned with and was expected to earn its keep. All horses, from the heavy draft-breeds to the lighter carriage, hackney and saddle horses, were kept for a purpose. I set out to report a part of our disappearing heritage and found instead that the horse's role, though diminished, is far from over. In the rural world the working horses, Clydesdales, Belgians and Percherons, still provide power for essential tasks as they did in the past. The pleasure horses, racers, hunters, jumpers and saddle horses, continue to fascinate today as they did in bygone days. I expected to find only memories of characters but instead I found people who work with horses in their daily lives. And they are a fine group.

It is to the people I met who shared my love and interest in the horse, and especially to the people in the book who let me come so freely into their lives, that this book is dedicated. And, of course, to the horses themselves.

A ride on Montreal's Mount Royal
in an old-fashioned calèche with
a brilliant sunset as backdrop is a
must for visitors, a tradition for
Montrealers.

# Introduction

When Columbus brought horses to the New World in 1493, he was in fact reintroducing horses to this continent. The horse family had flourished here many centuries before the arrival of Europeans. Fossil forms dating back some fifty or sixty million years suggest that the original 'horse' inhabited America when the continent was little more than dark forests and swamp wastelands. This small, roach-backed mammal, *Eohippus* (sometimes referred to as the Dawn Horse), bore little resemblance to his majestic descendants.

He was not much larger than a toy poodle; his front legs were shorter than his hind legs, and instead of the present-day hooves, he had toes – four on the front and three on the back. Such an awkward form might have served him well in pawing for his vegetarian diet, but it probably proved to be a hindrance to his speed and agility.

About thirty million years ago came the next major evolutionary step – *Mesohippus.* Although he actually differed little from *Eohippus,* he was slightly larger – about the size of a boxer dog – and had lost a toe from each foot. He still relied on forests and swamps for camouflage and food. Interestingly *Mesohippus* has been discovered only in North America; in Europe he is a missing link in the equine lineage.

By the time that primitive man was standing upright, *Mesohippus* had made way for *Phiohippus.* He was the size of a small donkey, no longer roach-backed, and the toes which had formerly adorned his feet were gone. His nose had elongated, and his legs had become stronger and more even. Now he could travel more swiftly and easily; thus he was able to avoid his enemies quite successfully.

About the time the ice age arrived, the true horse, *Equus caballus,* had evolved from *Phiohippus. Equus caballus* possessed most of the features recognized in the horse of today, and fossils show that many different varieties of the breed existed. Some were smaller than Shetland ponies; excavations made in Texas indicate that other strains could have reached a height of more than twenty hands. Other excavationary findings show man and horse connected around this period as hunter and hunted. However, the superior speed and agility of the horse, and the primitive state of man's weapons, ensured that the slaughter, such as it was, had little effect on the growth and development of the horse.

Suddenly about thirty or forty thousand years ago, the horse completely disappeared from North America. To this day its disappearance remains one of the great evolutionary mysteries. Speculation that a disease, such as equine sleeping sickness, caused the demise of the breed, is interesting but not convincing. Certainly sleeping sickness has caused havoc in horse-breeding areas in recent years, but it is unlikely that every last specimen on the entire continent would have been wiped out. Perhaps a combination of factors was at work: the ice age, diet, predators, disease. In any case, if his Eurasian brothers had not survived and maintained the species, the horse today would be as extinct as the dodo.

Exactly when man stopped hunting the horse and began to coexist with him is not known. Some speculate that this happened as long ago as 5000 B.C. in China or Mongolia. Others say that the first member of the horse family to be domesticated was the onager, or wild ass, used to pull carts by the people of the Fertile Crescent in the Near East. All we are certain of is that at some point the horse was domesticated, and a unique comradeship was established between horse and man. They became an almost invincible combination, exploring the world together, forming a working team that opened up greater possibilities than ever before. The gods of legend and folklore are often depicted on the backs of proud and august equines. And no wonder! No other animal has ever become so entwined in the development of mankind, nor deserved more the claim of being God-given.

At first horses were used mainly in tasks of war and combat. They would carry the saddles of Kings and of Emperors, and draw the chariots of armies into battle. There is record of Greek armies using chariots around 2000 B.C. and of mounted Asian warriors in the same era. Later, probably beginning in Northern Europe, the horse was put to work tilling crops and performing other mundane tasks. Men learned how to breed horses and produce blood strains suited to their needs and the environment. In the east the Arabian blood horse was bred for speed and sleekness; in the west heavier, stronger breeds were developed. The famous Shire horse of England owes its heritage to a decree by Henry VIII in 1541 that no stallion under fifteen hands high should be allowed to roam free in public parks or on common land. Henry, who was as well known for his unfailing eye for a good horse as for his unfailing eye for a beautiful woman, wished to upbreed the horses of his realm. He had in mind the heavy suits of armour worn into battle by his knights and the need for strong horses to carry the weight.

The French developed draft bloodlines, especially in Normandy, Brittany and La Perche, and fine high-stepping coach and saddle horses which they bred with great care. By the time the Americas were discovered, horse-breeding involving the most exclusive bloodstock had become the elaborate pastime of the elite. It was said that at this time, when royal courts and private kingdoms abounded, a man's place in society could be judged better by the blood in his stable than by the finery of his ladies' apparel. To call into question a man's knowledge of bloodlines was quite likely to provoke a duel.

In their conquest of Spain, the Moors had brought in a lighter, swifter, more agile horse than the larger walking horses preferred in northern Europe. This was the Arabian, the fabled forerunner of the modern racehorse, and the oldest known breed. After the Spanish had driven out the Moors, they combined Arab stock with heavier types to produce a horse suitable for herding cattle on their large stock ranches. It was this type of horse that Columbus brought to the New World on his second voyage in 1493. Thus the Spanish system of stock raising was introduced throughout the North American West, the Pampas and other areas of South America, and flourishes to this day with only minor changes. The horses of the Spanish conquistadors terrified the Indians. With horses and guns the Spanish were able to conquer Indian forces that enormously outnumbered them.

Possibly the first Indians to become accustomed to using the horse were those that worked at the Spanish mission-colonies established in the 1500s. The horse was a boon to the Indians of the Great Plains, for it enabled them to follow the buffalo on their migrations. Sedentary or semi-nomadic tribes became completely nomadic, often displacing tribes that had not yet acquired horses. The horse was a formidable war-machine, increasing the scale of conflict. Horse-stealing became a regular source of friction among bands, and cultural and social patterns were disrupted. The horse spread northwards from tribe to tribe, reaching the Prairies of Canada in about 1730. It is seldom realized that horses did not reach the Canadian Prairies until over a hundred years after the first horses had been brought from France to the struggling settlements of Acadia on the Atlantic coast thousands of miles to the east.

Horses in what is now Canada were initially brought from France by Poutrincourt in 1610 when he re-established the colony at Port Royal in Nova Scotia. More were brought by later settlers and some were lost to marauders from the British colonies to the south. But the Acadians never had large numbers of horses as they used oxen for farm work; their horses were for riding.

The first horse in New France was one imported to Quebec in 1647 for Governor de Montmagny; it does not seem to have survived long. In 1665, King Louis XIV of France sent a gift of twenty fine mares and two stallions from his Royal stables to the inhabitants of his new colony. Eight of the mares died on the rough Atlantic voyage, but the survivors were joined by another twenty-eight horses during the next five years. It is difficult to assess the exact bloodlines of these original horses, but they were mostly small rugged animals from Brittany and Normandy, relatives of the Percheron, and would probably have included some of the heavier drafts as well as the lighter breeds for carriages and riding. Apart from a few individual horses imported by the wealthier seigneurs, few other shipments to Quebec are recorded until after the British conquest.

When the first shipments of horses were received in New France, a breeding program was immediately put into effect. The mares were bred to the Royal stallions and when in foal they were rented to farmers, but they still remained the property of the King. The price for three years was one foal or 100 livres per horse per year. At the end of this period the horses and any remaining colts became the farmers' property. The foals gained by the Crown under this scheme were in turn bred and rented out to other farmers. The program was outstandingly successful, and by the turn of the century the number of horses exceeded seven hundred.

From this stock developed the first distinctly Canadian breed, the French-Canadian horse. The breed was not maintained in any especially scientific way. The horses were generally allowed to roam free and, as the stallions were not usually gelded, breeding was often uncontrolled. The general type that evolved was a sturdy work horse, good tempered, with sound feet, a small appetite, and, as might be expected, the ability to cope with Canadian winters. Sizes varied considerably, but the average height was about fourteen hands, the average weight was about 1200 pounds. The coat was rather rough and shaggy; the mane and tail thick, glossy and wavy. Valued for its sure-footed, high-tepping gait, the French-Canadian horse was used mostly for pulling the calèches in summer and carioles in winter when the habitants visited one another or went to church or market. It was also used for light farmwork and sometimes in multiple hitches for heavier work; but generally oxen were preferred for heavy work.

A popular pastime in those days was ice racing. At every possible opportunity, from small gatherings of friends to more formal festive occasions, the gallant French horses would gallop at full speed across the ice, racing cariole against cariole on the treacherous surfaces of river and lake. It was a common, and sad, sight to see horses with broken legs. Those who escaped the ice races unharmed were expected to stand steaming in the freezing winds, without blankets or covers, waiting patiently to pull the farmer and his family back to the homestead at full pace. Even on regular visits to neighbours, the habitants invariably drove recklessly at full speed.

Until late in the eighteenth century, the French-Canadian horse developed with little introduction of new blood from outside Quebec. After the conquest of Quebec, English-speaking settlers brought in the heavier draft breeds – Clydesdales, Suffolks, Shires and large horses from Vermont – that they were accustomed to use for heavy farmwork. The Loyalists brought French-Canadian horses to Upper Canada when they settled along the St. Lawrence and Lake Ontario in the 1780s. The French-Canadian thus was the foundation stock of the general work horses in Upper Canada, though it soon virtually disappeared as a distinct breed in Upper Canada through interbreeding with later imports.

Interbreeding with imported horses and heavy exporting to the northeastern United States ultimately led to the virtual extinction of the breed. The export trade began even before the American Revolution but it reached its peak after the American Civil War which consumed millions of horses. The burgeoning metropolises of the northeastern seaboard ran on horsepower, and the farmers of the St. Lawrence Valley were happy to sell their best stallions to the traders from the south, especially in years when crops failed and they had little other income.

Thus, by the end of the nineteenth century the breed in its pure form had just about disappeared. A society was formed for its preservation and examples best showing its characteristics were gathered. Its good qualities continue today in the Canadian horse, as it is now called, bred as a general purpose horse at a number of establishments in Quebec.

The story of the French-Canadian horse is told here because it is an intriguing piece of history that deserves to be better known. Perhaps because of its reputation as a poor man's horse, the French-Canadian's important place in the pedigrees of modern trotting and saddle horses is seldom recognized. It is an important ancestor of the Morgan and of other American breeds which owe their quick step and gentle disposition largely to the French-Canadian horse.

In Ontario and, later, in the West, oxen were often the first animals on the homestead. Slow, ponderous and dull, they nonetheless surpassed horses in brute stump-pulling strength and could live off grass, whereas horses required hay, oats and a shelter. The horse, however, was preferred by most settlers and would be bought as soon as finances allowed. As Grant MacEwan says in *Hoofprints and Hitching Posts,* "Many a settlers' shack heard the earnest prayer 'Please, Lord, spare my oxen . . . until I can get horses.' "

The average farm horse, of indeterminate breed and indifferent quality, led a hard life by today's standards, often with no reward but the slaughterhouse at the end. As Grant MacEwan has said, a monument should be raised

Harold Miller, his horse Molly and
a buggy repaired with baler twine
deliver the mail daily in the area
around Duntroon, Ontario.

to the pioneer farm horse. It would not "portray a prancing show horse with high head and swan-like neck and rounded body; rather, it would depict a dejected specimen with head held low, feet in the mud, ribs protruding pitifully and raw collar-sores on its scarred shoulders. It will not be an inspiring sight but it will be a reminder of what the pioneers' horses did in building a nation."

Indeed official concern about the quality of Canadian horses was frequently voiced. In 1886 Colonel F. G. Ravenhill toured the Dominion looking for remounts for the British cavalry. He found that Canadians, unlike their neighbours to the south, showed little enterprise in organizing horse markets and that commercial horse-breeding was largely dominated by American interests. He claimed that "the great proportion of horses met with of the size and sort suitable for British military purposes were unsound or blemished, from the farmers overworking their stock when too young. . . ." Of 7,674 horses examined, the Colonel and his mission bought 83. An Ontario committee in 1906 came to similar conclusions, finding that farmers sold off their best mares for quick money and bred from inferior stock. On the farmers' side it must be pointed out that the horse was a means, not an end, and few could afford to breed horses in the manner of landed gentry when survival itself was at stake.

In the same way that the car and all its associated industries seem to govern community life in the 1970s, so the horse dominated life in the nineteenth and early twentieth century. Business was assured for any blacksmith, wheelwright, coach-builder, saddler or harnessmaker who cared to set up shop. The veterinarian ranked as high as the doctor. Coachmen were employed for the countless hackney carriages and cabs, and many more men were engaged to drive the stage and freight lines. Every merchant owned a wagon or van and at least a couple of horses. Horses were everywhere – pulling the barges on the canals, powering ferry-boats, harnessed to the first streetcars and buses. Middle- and upper-class families had their riding horses, buggies and carriages. By the middle of the 1880s the streets of the cities were filled with the clamour and clatter of hooves and wheels rattling over the ruts. The din was every bit as great as that created by the automobile of today.

In smaller towns, the livery stable was the focal point of community life, more important even than the hotel or the town hall, more popular than the church or the saloon and certainly more entertaining than the theatre. Even in the smallest towns and villages there was a livery stable where men could rest and feed their horses while they shopped. It was there that you arranged to meet friends, make deals, settle arguments, or simply exchange gossip. In the smallest communities the stable proprietor was probably also the village blacksmith and harnessmaker. He would mend the farm plough or wagon and get new horses for the best possible prices. If there was no salesring or market, horse dealings were carried on in the local stable. The stable owner's word on the value of a horse was viewed with great respect, as was his general knowledge of community affairs. The livery stables were clearing-houses for gossip; newspaper editors frequented them in order to gauge public opinion, and politicians came there in order to try to change it.

The doors of the livery stable, like those of the church, were never closed, and the warm, friendly stove would seldom be allowed to go out. It was without question a man's domain – women and children had to wait patiently in a side room, or stand chatting to one another. Fortunes were made and lost within the walls of the livery stable; there, in the pungent scent of leather and straw, bets were placed and horses were bartered.

In the larger urban areas, the livery stable was a different proposition, specializing in the rental and stabling of horses and rigs. A variety of horses had to be provided, from the quietest of nags for the preacher to harness up to the buggy to visit his country parishioners, to an extra team of heavy horses for the lumber merchant to hire when required. In order to house such stock, the stable needed a large area, centrally located, and the price of such land was always at a premium. Yet obviously the stables flourished, because 41 stables were listed in the Winnipeg directory in 1909, and 52 stables were listed in Toronto in 1890. But this was not to last. By 1917 the number of livery stables in Toronto had declined to 31 and by 1930 to 4. The automobile had arrived.

Man and horse had become so closely associated over the centuries that the demise of the horse seemed impossible. Yet it was only natural that, once developed, the sputtering internal combustion engine would replace the horse. The battle between horse and engine was not, however, won quickly or easily. In 1903, the editor of the *Farm and Ranch Review* suggested, in defense of the horse, that "breeders had better cease worrying about the horseless age – which will only precede the manless age by a short time – and be on the lookout for the best stallions their means can afford for the coming season." This devotion to the horse was evident everywhere; society without horses seemed unthinkable.

Steam engines were the first to make serious inroads into the domain of the horse, but they were really only suited for working the machines of industry; as means of transportation they left much to be desired. Early gasoline-powered engines performed only a little better. Both engines required vast amounts of mechanical knowhow and patience; besides these early tractors and vehicles were painfully slow and heavy. On the streets they spooked the carriage-horses; on the land they became helpless in damp ground, and had to await the humiliation of being pulled out by a good draft team. Nevertheless the enthusiasts of these early engines shouted their praises loudly.

Then came the First World War. The horse went to war with man as it had for centuries. At home horses were worked harder to increase production; at war they had to risk their lives as cavalry mounts, hauling artillery and transports, or as general beasts of burden. Thousands met their death in the mud and artillery fire. Because of the war the horse suffered a major defeat! As has always been the way, the war gave technologists the opportunity to experiment. The combustion engine was developed and refined to power transports and machines of war, and the tank was invented. Motor power went to the front lines, and by the end of the war the horse was relegated to a secondary role.

After the war mechanization and mass-production increased rapidly. By the 1930s the streets and highways were crowded with automobiles and trucks. Some of the smaller merchant and delivery companies maintained their horses for a while but they were fighting a losing economic battle. The world of the working horse, and all that revolved around it, was doomed. There were too few horses for the blacksmith to make a living; the harnessmaker turned his talents to the upholstery of automobiles; the livery stable was replaced by the local gas station. In the country the defeat of the horse was slower, but it was just as certain.

Although cars and machines started to replace horses from the turn of the century, the horse population of Canada did not reach its peak until around 1921 when horses numbered about 3,600,000. The increase in the first part of this century is accounted for mostly by the development of large-scale farming using teams of heavy horses on the Prairies. The big changeover from horse-powered to engine-powered farming took place on the Prairies in the 1920s. The costly and magnificent teams of Clydesdales, Belgians, Percherons and other draft horses, bred with great care for the bloodlines and with great rivalry among partisans of the different breeds, soon became worthless. That farming practices on the Prairies courted the disaster of the dust torms has already been established; it remains for future historians to analyze the disruption of the rural economy by the debt-load that farmers were carrying as a result of converting from horse-power to engine-power. Ironically, farm animals were once again pressed into service to haul the Bennett-buggies of the Depression, the Model Ts that the farmers could not afford to repair.

Then another war unleashed its peculiar terror on the world, and everything that moved, it seemed, and much that did not, went to war. This time, however, horses were not needed at the front. But on the home-front, with fuel rationed and industry engaged in producing munitions, the horse was harnessed up again to haul wagon, van, plough, or harrow. With the coming of peace, the horse was once again redundant. Industry had changed its pace and the horse could no longer compete. In the country arable land was at a premium for food production and labour was in short supply. The new tractors and vehicles coming to market were refined machines that could do many times the work of a team of horses; they could be turned on and off at will and only needed one man's work to operate. Even the fodder and grazing needed by a horse was regarded as a needless extravagance. Only the nostalgic wealthy and the poor who had no choice kept, or wanted to keep, horses. The price of horses plummeted. With no buyers, the dealers went out of business. Horse-breeders stopped breeding and importers stopped importing. Even the small farmer, who had formerly kept a couple of mares in hopes of selling a colt each year at the fall fair, was forced to give them up.

The number of horses at the end of the Second World War was well over a million and their use of grazing was criticized by many. In 1945 the horse population in the western Provinces, largely unused and unwanted, had become such a burden that Government-supervised slaughterhouses and meat-processing plants were set up at Swift Current and Edmonton to supply the home market and the starving population of Europe with canned horse-meat. In the next decade some 300,000 horses, some from the best stock and bloodlines, were to end their days in this ignominious manner. Even on the small farms, where a man wanted to keep a team, love and memories had to be weighed carefully against the fifty cents a pound for horse-meat.

Certainly when Government grants and interest-free loans were being handed out to farmers who wanted to go with the tractor and gasoline (at the time cheaper than oats), sticking with horse-power seemed foolish and extravagant. The advantages of a tractor that could plough twenty acres a day, when even a good draft team could only manage about four acres, were difficult to deny. Besides, the farm equipment manufacturers had long since stopped making implements for horse power, and anything needed, like a plough or hay-rake, had to be found at farm sales and auctions.

The defeat of the working horse was not as complete in the eastern areas of Canada. Here many of the smaller farmers could not afford, or did not wish, to mechanize their operations; many who did change over to tractors found the payments and running costs too heavy to keep up. But nonetheless as old farmers sold up and died away, the working horses largely disappeared. In the logging industry horses remained in use for quite a while longer. In some areas, especially Quebec and the Maritimes, farmers until quite recently would supplement their meagre winter incomes by cutting and sledding trees with the help of their horses for lumber companies in areas where modern forest-harvesting machines could not work economically. But even here the price of a man's day has made this work unrewarding and Government benefit cheques have proved more appealing. In some of the smaller towns and villages merchants tried to keep on a horse or two for delivering their goods, but as housing projects spread ever outward the horse was retired in favour of the speedier truck.

Perhaps the greatest change in the rural world, besides the departure of the blacksmith, harnessmaker and carriage-maker, can best be seen at agricultural shows and country fairs. Where once farm owners and workers would have stood for hours discussing the virtues of a good mare or stallion, they now talk to the implement dealer about fuel consumption and repair costs or look at four-wheel-drive tractors, combine-harvesters and multiple-furrow ploughs. And the heavy horse show classes, the ploughing contests, the horse-pulls and the wagon-driving contests, once crowded with entrants, no longer attract enough contenders to take the prizes.

Along with the decline of the working horses has come a renewal of interest in the pleasure horses – hunters, jumpers and general riding horses. Undoubtedly one of the major contributing factors has been the international success of the Canadian equestrian team. They shone in the Olympics of 1968 and since then riding events have enjoyed greater coverage in the news media. Jumping, dressage and children bumping along on Shetland ponies have replaced the heavy horse-contests at rural fairs. Horse ownership is now on the increase; dealers and breeders are once again looking to the future with optimism. Riding schools and livery stables are springing up around major urban areas and people from all walks of life are discovering recreation and enjoyment in the old ways of the horse.

The heavy horses – the Belgians, Percherons and Clydesdales – are also becoming more popular, though now mostly with hobbyists or gentlemen farmers. At parades in cities and towns, at fairs, exhibitions and shows, the heavy horses, with their shining harness and heavy wagons, now draw the crowd's applause. More important though is the interest

Clydesdale mares and foals, some of the best stock being bred in Canada, on grazing land near Amherst, Nova Scotia.

shown once again in the horse as a practical working animal. Spiralling fuel costs are making farmers and farm managers look seriously at the economic virtues of a team, not necessarily to replace tractors, but to perform some of the tasks that are becoming too costly when done by machine.

At present this reintroduction of the working horse is only taking place on a small scale, but then again the high cost of energy and its ever-dwindling supply have only been evident for a few years. Many now view the use of horses on a modern farm with a skepticism similar to that which greeted the early traction engines and tractors. Change comes slowly to the rural world; but some are beginning to wonder, not whether the horse will outlive the age of the computer, but whether the computer will outlive the majestic power of the horse.

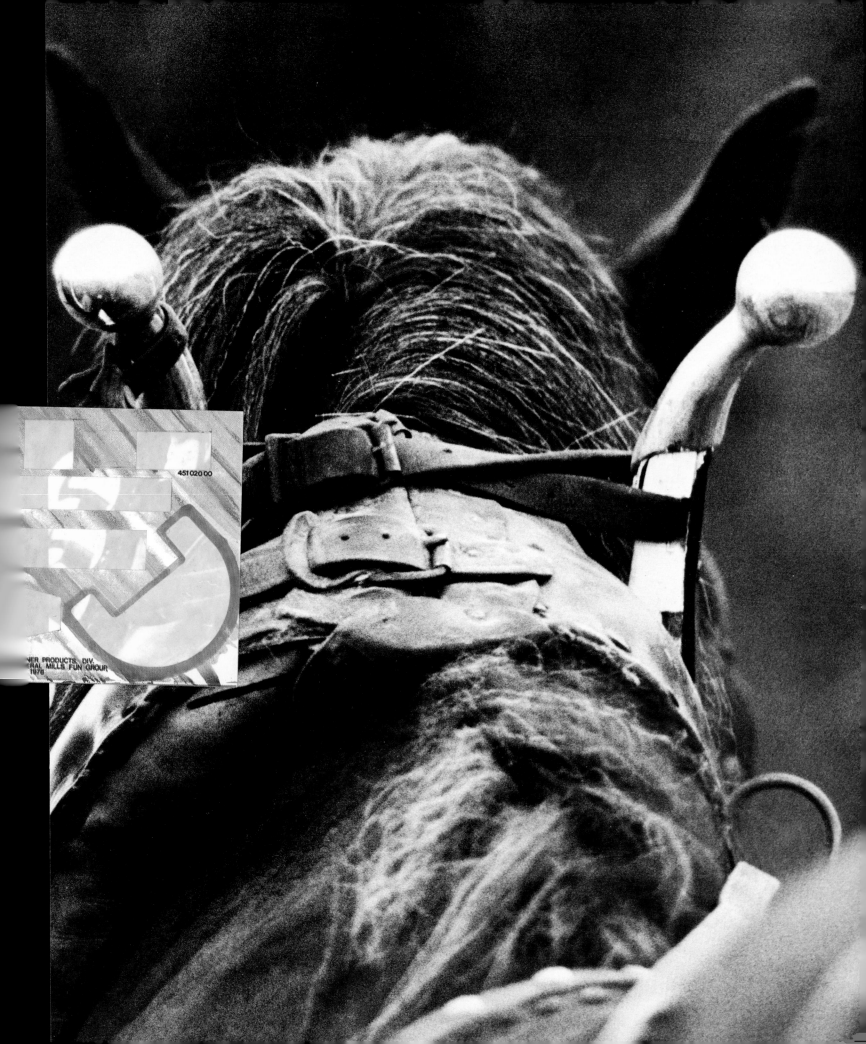

451020 00

NER PRODUCTS, DIV.
RAL MILLS FUN GROUP
1978

Just outside Sackville, New Brunswick, Dick McLeod puts his prized show-team of Clydesdales through some heavy fall ploughing. During the day he is a warden at the local prison, but in his spare time he likes to plough. Whenever a friend needs a bit of ploughing done, he is more than willing to offer his team.

Preceding pages. Farmer Ralph
Trentholm and his team haying
with an old hay-loader on the
Tantramar Marsh in Nova Scotia.
Below. Gladys Trentholm and one
of the horses hoisting hay up into
the barn.

# The Trentholms of Tantramar Marsh

Gladys Trentholm made me feel at home right away. She was that kind of country lady. Pleased to have visitors and friendly to strangers.

Ralph, my husband, will be back soon, but I don't think he'll be wanting to stop to chat now. He's down with the team in the marsh loading hay; you can see him from the fence behind the barn if you like. It's been a good year, this one. Good hay. The small barn is full already and most of the big one, and there's still a good lot to bring up. Ralph's been working late most evenings. In a while I'll have to leave you here and help him put the next load in the barn when he comes up.

While we waited, Gladys Trentholm took me into the living room and we talked over tea.

The Trentholm name has been associated with this area for a long time. Trentholms have been farming this bit of the Tantramar Marsh for three generations; we are part of the history of Nova Scotia. Some friends and I would like to write a book about this area some day if we get the time.

Ralph was born on this farm; not in this house we have now though, in the old one. The old house burned to the ground some twelve years ago. We were lucky not to lose the barns too – they were full of hay at the time. We did lose most of our personal things and heirlooms and that. For a while things were pretty hard for us but that's all behind us now.

The farm now has a hundred acres around it and another twenty acres for pasture down the road a bit. And we have thirty head of cattle. It's not a big farm, but it's a good one. Then Ralph delivers the mail around here too; that helps with the finances. That's become sort of tradition now; you see, he's been driving the mail for more than twenty-five years. That's every morning; after lunch he farms.

There's just the two of us on the farm now, working it. All we use for power is Joe and Riley, that's our team of Belgian geldings. Joe is a bit strong for me, a bit temperamental; but they're strong workers and go all right for Ralph. We used to have a tractor and machinery when Ralph's father ran

the farm, but when he retired Ralph went back to the horses. They are easier to work on the wet marshland without cutting up the soil like the tractor wheels do.

"My family still live nearby. Our son farms next door and helps us with the harvest; our daughter lives just down the road."

I wonder about their retirement plans from the farming life, but Gladys doesn't answer because Ralph has just come into the yard with his team and wagon. I am left drinking tea while Gladys goes out to help unload more of the good, sweet hay, made in the same way it has been made for three generations here on the Tantramar Marsh.

# Logging Horses

The way Queenie is able to manoeuvre through the thick underbrush, around the trees and stumps, without snarling her load is remarkable. Whether through instinct or experience, she knows her job and does it well. More importantly perhaps, working in the woods with ever-present danger, she knows when as well as how to do her work. But then things do tend to become second nature after a while, and Queenie has been working the woods for most of her nine years.

Queenie is a skid horse, or lumber horse, working in the forest areas around Plaster Rock, New Brunswick. She is part of a team; the other members are the men she works with. Queenie waits on the sidelines while the trees are felled and trimmed. When she is called she comes up, and the men hitch two or three twenty-foot logs to the chain behind her harness. She hauls or skids the logs to the place where they are stacked to wait trucking to the mill. Sometimes a man will walk with her and sometimes not, but the words spoken are few and the choice of path is her own.

Horses like Queenie were counted in their thousands in our woods at the beginning of the century. They were the backbone of the forestry industry. From coast to coast wherever trees were being cut horses were there hauling them. In the forests of British Columbia where men were cutting the huge pines and cedars that made the industry famous, horses worked in teams of a dozen or more, struggling with the heavy trees, hauling wagons loaded to breaking point along roughly made tracks, taking logs to the rivers and lakes so they could be floated down to the mills. The work for the horses here was hard and dangerous. On the steep inclines of the logging roads many a wagon over-ran its team and any serious medical attention was usually administered from a gun. For those that survived

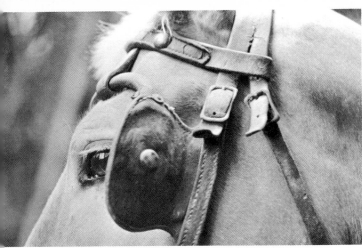

life was seldom enviable. Horses were treated with little more care than any other piece of equipment, indeed, often with less. In the best conditions they were housed in crudely erected shelters; otherwise they were merely tethered to trees. Except for what the horses could forage for themselves from the forest undergrowth, their fodder had to be brought in, with the result that they were frequently undernourished. The life expectancy of a skid horse was not great.

In the big lumber camps horses were owned by impersonal mills, but in areas where the woods were worked for the needs of the community horses fared far better. They were individually owned, purchased by men's savings, investments to be protected as long as possible. Usually they lived not in the woods where they worked but on farms, and when they weren't skidding logs they would be ploughing or bringing in the crops or taking the family on a picnic. . . .

Today skid horses have been replaced by tree-harvesting machines, but they did maintain their position of power long after tractors took to the fields. Indeed, up to a decade ago, horses were an important part of the equipment budget of even the largest forestry companies. Few companies own teams today, however; those that still use horses rely on freelance teams owned by local people. And, as usual, economic considerations make it unlikely that more than a handful of horses like Queenie will be working in the woods, sharing the life of the lumberjack, by the end of the 1970s.

# Historic Farm

Orwell Corners is a rural crossroads village on Prince Edward Island, just twenty miles outside Charlottetown. There are many similar communities on the island, but Orwell Corners is different in that it is run on the day-to-day methods of the mid-eighteen hundreds.

The people of Prince Edward Island are proud and protective of their heritage. Agriculture is at the heart of the island's economy. And at the heart of its agriculture is the traditional, small, family-run farm and the closely-knit village life. Recently, however, tourism has become the second most important industry of the island, and with the tourists have come all kinds of changes. Many islanders fear that their special way of life, with its inherent colour and fascination, is changing and disappearing. Orwell Corners attempts to preserve some of the more interesting old ways.

Gathered together on a few acres are a church, schoolhouse, country store and post office, farm house and barns. All painstakingly restored, they create the atmosphere and appearance of a century ago.

Orwell Corners also has a team of horses, a magnificent matched pair of Belgians. They are popular with visitors as part of the village, but they are also a practical addition in that they work daily on the small farm. Around and in the barns can be found old farm implements and wagons, all in working order and used on the fields. But hay is the major crop, and the horse-drawn hayrides please the tourists most of all. The horses do, however, offer more than just entertainment. Working the land as they do, they offer a sight of horse power, the working power used by man for centuries, and now almost gone.

Opposite page. An old buggy meticulously restored in front of the barns at Orwell Corners. Left. A set of discs being hauled to work one of the farm's fields.

Preceding pages. Johnny McLeod
of Prince Edward Island ploughing
with his Percheron team in the early
fall.

# Johnny McLeod's Percherons

Johnny McLeod is a small man, quiet and tidy. He didn't mind talking but he had to change into clean shirt and overalls before any photographs and he had to finish the chores before afternoon tea. With his wife he lives on the farm his father bought in 1903. Situated in the St. Peters District of Prince Edward Island, with only about half of the hundred acres cleared, the rest being good woodland, the farm is not big, but it is cared-for, kept in repair and the fields have been nurtured to give the best the rich red soil can offer. Johnny works alone, and although he has an old tractor and a few modern implements for the heavier chores, it is his beloved team of Percherons that he uses mostly.

"It's like anything you get used to," he explains. "You've had it all your life and you just get attached to it."

Ever since he can remember in his sixty plus years, Johnny has worked with draft horses.

"When I was a little kid my father always liked me to drive the horses, you know. I learned right from the time I knew anything, I guess. He would put me on the horses, the backs, and he would be going back and forth to the fields to work, so I guess I learned from there.

"He died in 1951, but I had been running the farm for quite a few years before that, around ten years or more before that. I just stayed home with him and gradually took over as he got old and not able to do the work. I guess by that time I was really used to working the farm with the horses then."

Back in the days before the Second World War horses were essential on the land in this part of Canada. Tractors were considered new-fangled and viewed with great skepticism. Days seemed slower then, with longer hours. Harvest time meant neighbours going together from farm to farm to help get in the wagon loads of sweet hay, thresh the corn and dig the root crops. In the winter the days were filled with chores around the farm, feeding the stock and working in the woods, cutting and skidding the logs for winter warmth and spring fence-work.

"Sometimes in the bad weather, when we were kids, they would take us to the school in a horse and sleigh. We all used to like that, you know. It was fun. Yes, years ago it was sleighs for everything in the winter. Anywhere you went it was by sleigh. After a storm it was pretty bad for a horse. But after a few trips everybody got travelling, and the road would be down and you could get along nice like. We drove into Charlottetown a few times, that was maybe thirty-five miles. That was a good day, we used to stay overnight and come back the next day.

"Sometimes we used to go on picnics with a team and the farm wagon. The whole family used to go. My father used to take the horses and drive them. They were Sunday School picnics mostly. Of course, anyone around who wanted to go was welcome. There's none now; we don't go anyways.

"I'd go into ploughing contests sometimes, you know, still do sometimes, not as much though. I was in my late twenties when I started ploughing competitions. The first time I was the fastest and I knocked third out of it in my class. It wasn't bad for the first time. Sometimes I'd be second or third, and sometimes, once in a while like, first. But the hardest competitor we had, he doesn't plough now, so I got a little better chance of getting first or second.

"The first time I went into competition there were maybe thirty teams. Now there's only maybe half a dozen. But I get a lot of kick out of it myself. Mind you, it's hard on the back now. You got to tie the reins around your back and lean back on them so it leaves your arms free for the plough handles. But it pulls on your back a good deal. I take a lot of pride in furrowing though, ploughing just in the field. That's the way you've got to practice.

"It would be no trouble for me to plough two and a half, three acres a day. That's with the two furrow plough. With the one furrow, in the old days, I'd work a long day and figure maybe an acre and a half. That was good ploughing. It depended on your team, you know. You have to have a good team for ploughing. I think the furrow horse is, well, it's very important that you have a good furrow horse. Of course, the other one's got to be good too. If they don't go even and steady they start going crooked on you; it's pretty hard to do very much with them then. The ones I've got now are a good team, good workers, very even-tempered they are. Mind you, you can't be in a bad mood with them either. They feel it, you know, and get scared and froth up. They are not as stupid as people think they might be.

"I still use the horses for just about everything around the farm. This spring I sprayed the fields out the back and spread manure. We used to use three horses hitched for that, but I've done it with the two. It's a bit slower though. The other day I had a big roller here to roll the grain in. That was four acres; the roller makes a nice clean job of it. Last winter I cut fourteen cord of wood and hauled it in by myself, with the team like. I'll put it this way, the horse still has a place on the farm today, I think, at least it has for me but maybe not for too many.

"I really feel bad to see them go out so much from use. They started to go out about twenty-five years ago around here. That's when the tractors came in. Then most people who kept them on got too old to work them, I guess, and the horses just stopped. There's very few young people now who care too much for horses. They wouldn't know how to harness one up, never mind work a team.

"The major problem with working them is the equipment. Most things you can't get today. Nobody much is making anything for the horses. I just use the old ones I have and that'll do me. I do all my own repairs, mainly on an old forge I picked up somewhere. I got all the tools and that for the blacksmithy work as well, the horse-shoeing like.

"Yes, I'd be really lost without them. Some never care if they see a horse; but me, I do. I tell you truthfully, if I couldn't keep at least one horse around me I couldn't stay here. I'd give it up, truthfully."

# Collecting the Irish Moss

When the seas storm on the north-western shores of Prince Edward Island, the famous red sands become a hive of activity as virtually every member of every local family gets out to gather the seaweed cut loose by the sea's rage. The seaweed, called Irish moss, is found only in a few places in the world and nowhere as abundantly as in this part of Prince Edward Island. Although Irish moss looks and feels much like any other sea crop, it possesses an emulsifying property that makes it useful in the manufacture of over a thousand products ranging from ice-cream to tooth paste to automobile tires. Its discovery and harvesting has brought economic benefits to the area.

The methods used to collect the moss are simple and efficient. What is washed ashore is merely gathered up by rake and fork and loaded onto wagons. But for what is left floating in the waters horses are brought in. And with the horses come the children. A large metal rake or scoop is harnessed behind a horse, and a child of suitable age and strength is placed on his back to steer him. Then the pair go trotting or cantering along the shallow ebb waters raking up the moss behind them. When the scoop is full, it is dragged onto the sand, emptied and off go the enthusiastic pair for more. Later the seaweed is spread out to dry in the sun and taken by horse and wagon to the processing plant where it is baled up and sent to places the world over.

Although the Irish moss industry is only fifteen or so years old and hence came into being in this mechanized age, the horse is the power source for the families who collect it. The reason is economic. This has always been a fishing and farming area. Thus every family had at least one working horse. The fishermen used horses to haul in the boats and take the catch to market. The farmers, and most families both fished and farmed, used horses in the fields. When the moss business came along, they naturally used the power easiest to hand. Besides, if a tractor gets out a little too far in the water and a wave hits, there is trouble, but a horse just shakes his back and keeps on going.

# Weir-fishermen of Fundy Bay

In the part of Nova Scotia where the Lewis brothers live, near the Five Islands in the Bay of Fundy, the tides often reach a height of twenty-five feet. Although few have tested the theory, the tides are said to come in faster than a man can run. Such tides, which one day may be harnessed to provide hydro-electric power to the Maritimes, make possible a method of harvesting fish, called weir-fishing, which is unique to this part of Canada and which has been practised here for generations.

The Lewises are pretty well the last weir-fishermen still working the waters. Each spring they, like generations before them, go into the woods along the shore to cut brushwood. Loading it onto the wagon behind their nine-year-old gelding, Tom, they haul it out at low tide for maybe two miles across the wet, red sands to the place where they want to build their net. They have the fishing rights to this part of the Bay and seldom build in the same place two years running. They don't know whether fish are intelligent and don't care really; it's just that you never build the same place twice in a row.

Usually building the net takes six to eight weeks, longer if it's a stormy spring, and untold trips with Tom and the wagon. The Lewises stake and weave each load, much like basketmakers working at their craft; and, when they finish they have a semi-circular fence or net some three-quarters of a mile long, fifteen feet high in the centre and tapering off to five feet at the ends. God and the tides willing, the net will last the summer and fall without needing too many repairs.

The way the weir-net works is very simple. As the fast Fundy tides rush in, bringing the fish, water covers the nets by maybe forty feet; then when the tides ebb, the fish are trapped behind the net and the Lewises just walk out with their horse and wagon to pick the fish off the sands or net them out of the shallow tidal pools.

Over the years the tides have changed, the catches diminished and an impersonal, mechanized fishing industry has replaced weir-fishing. Some weir-fishermen tried at first to mechanize the industry by using tractors instead of horses to build and maintain bigger net areas. But after a couple lost their tractors to the rushing tides, most of the others gave up.

Nowadays only the Lewises remain and they couldn't afford a tractor even if they wanted one, which they don't. They figure Tom will do them for a while; when he gets too old to walk the sands, they too will give up the fishing. And another part of Maritime tradition will pass into history.

# Jack MacKenzie, Harnessmaker

The Sackville Harness Shop on Main Street in Sackville, New Brunswick, has been in operation for about fifty years. The heavy horse harness made there, and especially the handmade, straw-filled collars that Jack Mackenzie makes in the back room, are famous throughout the continent. Soft-spoken and rather shy, Jack sat surrounded by straw and leather as we talked about harness making.

"I've been in the business, oh, about thirty-six years now, making horse harness. Making the collars all the time. I'm what you'd maybe call a collar-man. But I've not got tired of it yet. Oh, I get a little tired of just sitting down all the time out the back here, you know. A little weary sometimes, but never really discouraged. No. I still get a lot out of making a good collar.

"I make collars here, and the harness we make we send out all through the Maritimes here and down into Ontario and America there. You know, I made collars for that Budweiser forty-horse team. Yes, I made the collars and they put that fancy polished facing on. We used to make some show facings like that here, but there isn't the call now or the time so we stopped doing it. But we sell other things. We had a young girl in here making leather bags and we sold them and the belts. Then we sell saddles and blankets and supply a lot of smaller outfits with leather and hardware for them to make harness. Things are going good at the moment. No complaints really.

"A fella should be able to make a collar in a day, to make it right. It takes a good time because you have to fill the straw tight and even, you see. That's with the big collars, for the big drafts like the Belgians and Clydesdales. The smaller collars, for ponies and that, well, you could maybe make two in a day.

"I use this long rye straw. Now that's not too common now, not with the combines chewing it all up. We have ours grown special down the way a bit. They thresh it there for us and keep it long. That way you get a better harness. If you fill harnesses with short straw, like the machine ones, they lose their shape; and if the covering gets torn, the straw falls out. The long straw keeps its shape and you can repair it easy. I use a ton and a half of that straw through the year.

"There's a fair lot to a working harness, you know, and we make it all here and near all of it is hand-worked. There's the bridle and reins, then there's the pad that fits on the horse's withers and the birching that goes on the rump. The girth holds the padding on and the tugs go along the side of the horse there and hook onto the hames on the collar, and that pulls the load. It sounds sort of strange at first, I suppose, but you soon learn when you're working with it.

"This line of work here, there used to be a harnessmaker in near every village and there was more than enough work to go around as well. That was a good time ago now though. This shop, it was opened in nineteen-twenty, I believe, and then it was pretty well all horses around here. That changed twenty or thirty years ago, after the war, I suppose. The horses started to go out, off the land. There weren't the horses and so there wasn't the use for a harnessmaker. A good many shops closed then. I knew a number myself. But they couldn't, you know, keep going. It was pretty tough around here in the fifties, the early fifties.

"Now, well now, there is this new interest with the draft horse. We see it here. People who have a liking for the older times and horses and that, and maybe buy a team to show at the fairs. And there again, a lot of the horses are being used back on the farms. That maybe has something to do with the gas prices, I suppose, but we get a lot of orders for working harness. Mind you, there are a good number of shops around, saddle and leather shops, that can make you a harness. But, well, as far as these straw collars, I'm the only one around as far as I've heard that does it. The only one on the continent maybe.

"Now I've got this young man starting up with me next month. He's going to learn collar-making, going to be a collar-man like me. Learn the harness-trade like. That's nice, you know. I'd like to see it carried on.

"It's difficult to keep up with the orders people want now though. We've had to turn work down; we're that busy. Now I'm sixty-one come September and, well, I don't know that I'll keep on doing it much longer. It's hard work, you know. It's busy here. Paul Blakeney, the manager here, the man who has the shop with me, he was poorly last year a while, and, well, I hope we can get some people in to carry it on. I wouldn't like to see it close up. You know, it becomes a part of you, working with smelling the leather and that. I guess I'll miss that a bit when I give it up."

The Sackville Harness Shop in Sackville, New Brunswick, is one of the last on the continent to specialize in handmade harness.

# Maritime Cowboys

Cowboys are seldom associated with the Maritimes, but on some of the newer intensive beef-rearing units men with horses have been added to do the cow-work. On the Dundas Farms in Prince Edward Island, a big cooperative where large numbers of the French Charolais cattle are being bred, the men who work the cattle have some of the best cutting and saddle horses in the country. And although they haven't adopted the traditional dress of their Western counterparts, these Maritime cowboys have gained all the skills of cattle herding.

# Western Parade

Everybody loves a parade, of course, and no one more than the people of Calgary and Edmonton. In Calgary the big event is the annual Stampede Parade; in Edmonton it's the parade on the Klondike Days celebrations.

The west has a special love and respect for horses as its growth and prosperity have depended greatly on them. Horses turned the prairies into wheat fields, hauled the forest logs of the lumber industry, helped build the railroad and the oil rigs, pulled the wagons and herded the cattle. And they made many men rich.

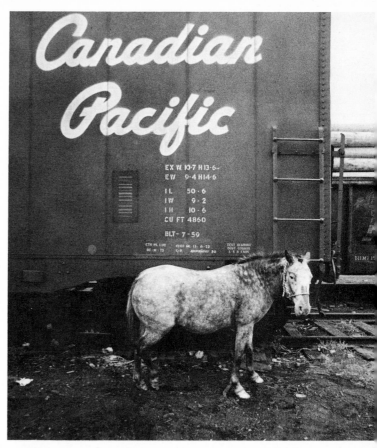

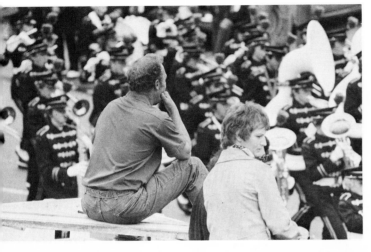

# Western Horses

t the time when the great railroad was being pushed across
e country, horses were running as a feral breed through
uch of the land. Eventually they were herded, bred and
t to work for the cowboys. Some ranches boasted two
d three hundred horses. The Douglas Lake Ranch was
id to have that many heavy horses alone. The number of
rses was impressive indeed, as was their wild beauty.

oday in the west every horse has an owner, as does every
w. But does the fact that no "wild" horses run the ranges
ese days really matter much? The number of horses is
aller today and the sighting of a herd less frequent, but

the horses are of no lesser stock. They are of highly-bred
and priced quarterhorse and thoroughbred bloodlines. Free
to roam the high summer pasture, they gain their ground
footing, learning the skills of fast turns and anxious stops,
the very requirements that will be made of them as working
saddle or cutting horses.

Horses near Nicola Lake and
Merritt in British Columbia

The round-up barbecue on the
Capps' ranch in southern British
Columbia.

# Round-up Barbecue

For as long as there have been cattle and fall round-ups
in the west, it has been the custom of ranchers to host annual
ranch barbecues. These are as traditional to the cowboy
as his Stetson or fresh corn on the cob.

The preparations start in the last days of summer. A couple
of good steers are picked out for slaughter and a pit is dug
for the fire. At the more formal affairs johnny-on-the-jobs
are erected; at others signs are put up directing traffic to
solitary clumps of trees. This is the men's work. The
neighbourhood women are regimented into teams to bake
cakes, pies, cookies and bread. And the local square-dance
musicians get out their fiddles and guitars to rehearse their
repertoire of tunes.

Everyone around is invited; any that are missed know that
they will be welcome anyway, such is the informality of
the west. The great day arrives. Tables are put out and
covered with the home-made delights. An old bath-tub or
three are filled with beer. Logs and planks are placed about
as seats.

The guests arrive on foot, in cars, trucks and, of course,
on horseback. Mums and Dads with children in tow. Young
men and women prettied up for the dancing. Grandparents
who have been to many functions like this and have that
look of mischief in their eyes that says they will be children
again before the night is over.

First come the helloes, the back-slapping, the hand-pump-
ing, the exchange of yarns and gossip. Then it's time for
a drink or two and a bite to eat. A few necessary speeches
are made to calm the digestion, and finally the dancing
and general shindigs take over. Friendliness is the key, and
no one is friendlier than the rancher saying thanks to his
workers.

The idea is to stay on for ten seconds. It seems a short time really, but to the bronco-rider it is a lifetime. When the horse comes out of the shute it is wild, the pinching surcingle around its flank driving it to buck with a frenzied cruelty far beyond its normal desire to throw off the rider. And the wilder the horse, the better the cowboys and the crowd like it. Skill is as much a part of the game as staying on for ten seconds. Certainly if the rider hits the ground before those seconds are up, he is out of the running; but if he rides without style, he is out of the fame.

Of course, any good rodeo offers other attractions also. The dances and partying, the midway and Ferris wheels, and the ever-present hamburger stands create a carnival atmosphere. But the cowboys and their families are the real reason for visiting a rodeo. They are the modern-day nomads, living their lives from the backs of camper trucks, driving from rodeo to rodeo. When they arrive a small town seems to spring up overnight. With their horses tied to car-door handles, fenders and wing mirrors, they are oddly reminiscent of the wagon-trains of old. It is a close knit community with a unique way of life, perhaps comparable only to the car-racing fraternity. In both sports death and injury are always expected, always accepted.

There are other events at the rodeo as well: the Brahman bulls, the chuck-wagon races, steer-wrestling that has left many a cowboy with a horn in his ribs and calf-throwing that is guaranteed to ruin an overzealous back. But it is the bronco-busting that draws the entries and the crowds to applaud them.

The ultimate distinction is to ride at the Calgary Stampede. But to enter here a rider must already have proved himself at countless smaller rodeo events held throughout the west. He will probably have a good number of scars and broken bones and might be starting to wonder if it is really worth the trouble and pain. But if he is good, really good, doesn't break another bone and comes out first, he will be about twenty-five thousand dollars richer at the end of the year. If not, he might have to sell his soul for the next entrance fee.

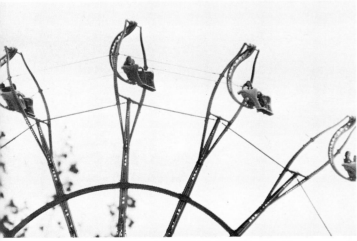

Calf-roping at the Calgary
Stampede tests both the cowboy's
roping skills and his quarter horse's
ability to reach full gallop and come
to a complete stop all in a few
seconds.

# Cowboy Horse

A cowboy lives on his horse. From before dawn to early dusk, he and his saddle horse are virtually inseparable. Legends about the cowboy horses of the western ranches in the past are as varied as they are numerous. A cowboy was a roamer. He had few possessions and shared most of them, but no one ever took a man's horse without asking. Men died for less. The ranchers grew rich feeding and breeding cattle on the ranges, and it was the cowboy's horse that made the ranges workable. Actually the cowboy's life has changed very little today. He still lives the bunk-house life-style, and his day-to-day work still includes the round-ups, the branding, the calving and always the fence-work.

In recent years many of the larger corporate-run ranches have turned to trucks and land vehicles and two-way radios. Others use helicopters and snowmobiles. Modern, polluting, high-pressure methods have come to the west. But on most ranches the horse still does the cow-work. The sight of a cowboy and his cutting horse working in the corral, darting this way and that, edging a calf from the herd for branding, or turning a stray back on the cattle drive to summer pasture is every bit as thrilling as the beauty of dressage. For the time being, at any rate, this legendary figure on horseback will continue to tend cattle on the range.

# Herb Heintz

"We've just the two horses. That bay one, Barney, I think we had him about four years now. The other one, Dan, we bought two years ago. I had a whole bunch of other horses but none to go with that bay. I had him weighed a year and a half back, just to see like. Eighteen-hundred pounds he weighed, and he's real strong. The other one is a little heavier, maybe two thousand pounds, but there's not the same spirit. They make a good work team though, real good. I don't really need another team, not yet a while.

"We get going steady in the woods down the way and across the fields maybe seven, eight hours most days. It's wet going, underfoot like, gets real marshy sometimes. We're out there cutting trees, spruce and pine mainly, for logs. We cut six and a half and eight-foot ones. They're best for fence-work. Anything big we cut for gate-posts like. Last year we cut and sold near a hundred and fifty thousand posts. It's not a bad business. It's been a good year, this year, steady.

"We had some fellas up here working for us a while ago and they had Barney in the bush with them, making posts. And every load he'd haul out they got a hundred posts out of it.

"Our whole family lives around here pretty well. Have since Dad bought the old farm in 1938. I grew up on the farm, not here like, but down the road. Ever since I could drive I've had to work with them, I guess. It's rough farming around here. I used to work them in the fields, since I was around thirteen, ploughing and that. And I used to take the wagon on the chores. We were about four miles from the store and with the horses we would tramp out across to the store for groceries and back home. It was half a day to relax. Now, you know, we go to the same store in just a few minutes with the truck. But back then we never went anywhere else much, only where we could take the horses.

"I guess there are a lot of memories of being children, like with the horses. Actually that's partly why we still have them, work with them like . . . we always had them. Doreen and I been married fifteen years now and we always had a team around us. That and the economical side also. There is a place up the road a way, like mine, same operation, fence-posts. They just got this big Caterpillar; $18,000 they paid for it. Well, when you start talking that kind of money these small places don't work. You can't afford tractors like that and make any sort of profit. Besides, they still get stuck in the snow.

"And then they're talking of putting another rise on the cost of a gallon of gas. You can't do it. Least I don't see it. Some of these big ranchers now are buying teams to do the chores and in the winter you get a lot of them use a team and sleigh for feeding the stock. At thirty below a tractor don't want to start, you know, but a horse, well, he don't mind it none, not with a good feed in him. I don't think there'll ever be a time when I get rid of them, except maybe if I get too old. But you always need a team around for the choring and to get out into the woods.

"Mind you, finding equipment now for working with them on the land is getting difficult. I go to the sales myself and farm auctions and pick up what I can. I got a rake a while back for five dollars. I guess every time a sale comes up it's another small farm like mine gone out. They get too greedy, some do. They want anything that's bigger and better and needs less work. Me, I work hard, six, seven days a week. It's a long day but it's O.K. if you don't mind.

"I like it this way, working with the horses. You don't have to worry about them like you do a tractor. Besides they get to know what they have to do and most of the time don't need you to tell them anything much except to start and stop. I guess often they even know that better than you do."

Herb Heintz, who cuts and sells fence posts, working with his horses on his land near Carrot Creek, Alberta.

# Mel Heintz, Horse-dealer

To Mel Heintz horses are a way of life. He has earned considerable respect in the Alberta area for his eye for a good horse. As a dealer and breeder he handles some excellent stock. His prize Belgian stallion, King, has sired many strong colts in the growing demand for heavy horse stock in the west. Mel Heintz also uses his horses for working his farm. Chores that his horses perform include cleaning the driveway in winter with an old road-grader and feeding the thoroughbred stock in winter pasture.

# Blacksmith

Blacksmith Jon Martin in his shop
in St. Jacobs, Ontario.

"As far as the horse-shoeing is concerned, here we still do some, but not a lot now. I must say, I don't do any myself. Not now for a year last February. I got injured shoeing a horse actually. Got my leg, kicked out like. Well, I can get around pretty good now but I've been doing this kind of work for forty-eight years close now, and I think a fella should slow down a bit, take things a little easier. So I have a young lad, a blacksmith like, and he comes in once or twice a week and does the shoeing.

"There aren't as many horses around this area now. We've got so close to the cities. Waterloo there, now that's only two miles down the road, give or take a little to the city limits. Because of this I reckon most of the horse workers have been crowded out of the area.

"But we've been trying to keep up the old blacksmith shop. Keep it in shape, the appearance and that. Try to present the old time work, the old time attitude of a shop like this one.

"Now in most cases a horse will come in and have a set of shoes put on and he'll be away. Well now, maybe you don't see him again for six, eight, maybe ten weeks and by that time the shoes are worn down. The heels like, and the corking on the toes. You ask a few questions about how he's been working, travelling and that, and then you add all this together before you start to shoe him. As far as the horse-shoeing business is concerned, there's quite a difference between picking up a horse's foot and nailing a shoe on it and actually shoeing, a lot of difference. To know the foot, know the hoof and how to trim it and what it needs done to keep it healthy. Knowing the bones of the horse, their structure, and that sort of thing. It's very important to the acual shoeing and you have to be able to size it up when you shoe the horse. Then there is the shaping of the shoe and fitting it properly. Maybe you have to change the type of shoe to make the horse travel better. It all takes time; it takes years to observe what a certain kind of shoe will do to a horse. You have to look close, observe, experiment with different shoes for different problems. Maybe you get a horse in that is different, difficult to shoe like. Well, you have to be able to shoe it right, else you'll be wasting your time. That isn't something you learn in a few weeks like some reckon. You can't learn to shoe a horse using dead hooves for teaching. You have to work on a live horse, one

that's working. You have to know him, care about him. That's what shoeing horses is really.

"Now these pleasure horses, hobby horses as I used to call them, that you get around these days, shoeing them is easier. They do nothing but a little walking and trecking and don't go on the roads very much. Well, as long as they have a shoe fitted so that they protect the hoof like, stop it from cracking, well, that's all right, I suppose.

"But when you get a horse that's working all day, maybe travelling some thirty or more miles along the hard tops here, well, that is something altogether different. Then you have to have good shoes and have them properly fitted. A horse can't work to it s best if it isn't well-shod.

"You know, there's quite a few kinds of shoes. Standard ones and that, and specialized ones for when a horse isn't walking right. He might be wearing down one side of the shoe too much or be walking uneven. Well, you wouldn't want to fit just any old shoe there; you'd use a special one like people use special shoes sometimes to help them walk. Well, it's the same with horses.

"Most cases a steel shoe will last the biggest part of a year, being properly cared for, taking them off regularly, repairing them and that. For the good of the horse they should be taken off the hoof every, oh, eight weeks or so. Then you trim the hoof back, repair, rework the shoe and then re-fit it.

"We usually use the hard-faced shoe now. It's harder wearing. There is a tungsten carbide surface and we put the corking on here. It's a better shoe, I think. Now for a set like that, fitted and all, we charge twenty-six dollars. I'll tell you, back in thirty-two when I started out here, in the business, I was getting twenty-five cents a shoe for a re-set, and fifty cents for new ones. It's changed a bit, you could say, I suppose.

"A shoe should be strong so that it protects the hoof. Supports it like, keeping it sturdy. It's like walking on gravel in sneakers, the thin sole doesn't protect your foot and it gets sore. Well, it's the same for a horse. If the shoe isn't right it hurts.

"I don't make the shoes anymore. I could, I suppose, but there's no need. The ones we use here, the hard-faced ones, are good shoes. It's good quality steel; they last a long time. We get them from an outfit in Minnesota. Been getting them there since I can remember. That's the only place I know of anywhere in America that makes shoes, and there's no place at all in Canada.

"Now I'll tell you something. We sell this other shoe here and it's made in Japan. Yes, Japan. This is the beautiful thing. We Canadians, you know, we're so smart. We don't want to bother with all the old cars and scrap that is piling up acres all over the place. No. It gets loaded on ships to Japan. They get it ground up, smelted up, and re-worked and that, and then we go over there and bring it back as horse-shoes. I don't see why, with the unemployed, the welfare and people without very much money and that, why can't it be done here. What's the reason? Now that is what I call smart, real smart. And I'll tell you this, as far as I am concerned, these shoes are not much cheaper and not as good; they break at the nail holes often.

"This forge here now, well, I just sold it up a while back. I'll keep running it, mind. After the accident there, back when I got injured, I didn't know whether I would be able to do much. I just put up a little "For Sale" notice in the window here. I wasn't too worried about selling it too quick. Some people from around here – they have this restaurant – good, nice people, they bought it. They reckon it gives character to the village here. The people, you know, tourists and the like, they like the old blacksmith shop, I suppose. Well, that's fine.

"But I'll keep on working here. There's still a lot of work around for a blacksmith. I'm reasonable healthy, I think, and as far as work goes I can keep going a while yet. As far as this line of work goes, in a shop like this where we do a little manufacturing of tools and repairs and that, it gets hot, heavy, and rough. You get pinched, burned, bruised and that. If you drop a piece of iron on your foot or finger it's hard and heavy, not like wood. The sparks from the forge welding will burn holes in your eyeglasses. But I've always enjoyed it, still do as far as that goes. Still do.

"Now I'm not what you might think of a blacksmith much. Most people and the movies talk about the big, robust, hefty blacksmith, you know. Well, I've never weighed more than a hundred and forty-five pounds and, like I said, I've been shoeing now for forty-five years. At the present time I don't even weigh a hundred and thirty pounds.

"The horses today aren't treated anywhere near as good as in the old days. Now, today most of the horses on the farms aren't being used that much, just for the chores and that. Well, I think in many cases, and I know some, the horses are really neglected sometimes. There are a few around that do take care and time to treat their horses like they deserve. And a horse will always work better for you if you treat it right and give it a bit of loving, you know. Mostly though, well, they just think of him as another piece of machinery. Turn it off and forget about it. They don't care much. You see, they see the horse as unproductive. They're not like the hogs, fattening cattle and that. They don't bring in the dollars, and they get treated in that sort of neglect. It's sad really. I don't like to see it. Earlier when the horse was really productive you really took care of him. If you didn't, you'd lose him or your job.

"You know, there used to be a lot of competition among blacksmiths, not in contests so much, like at shows and fairs, but real competition. Between fellas like, with shops all in one area. There is still a little today but not like it was. Oh no. Back in the early years when I started there were a lot more shops like this one around. Every village and hamlet had one at least. Even here in St. Jacobs, which was much smaller then, there was three outfits just within a few doors of each other. You could see just what the other fella was about, what business he was doing, what customers he had and all. This was the common thing of course; this was the competition. There were a couple of brothers up near Heidelberg way, they both opened up shops and, let me tell you, they were real competition, real opposition, you might say. They both of them thought they knew better than the other, and both said they were right.

"It's changed today though. There aren't the same pressures. If someone needs a blacksmith shop there aren't many around for him to choose from, are there now. But in those days your business depended on your work, your skill, knowing something, some trick that the other fella didn't know. And you made sure he didn't find out either. That was the real competition."

# Auction

The atmosphere is distinctly country. The faces show the lines of weathering as only the faces of country people do. The clothes are country from the worn but polished boots to the angle of the caps. And here and there bits of straw are being thoughtfully chewed in friendly mouths. These are farm people; they know it and are proud of it. Talking among themselves they seem not to notice the city folk looking on like an audience at a theatre. But then this is the heavy horse auction, the domain of the farmer, and the men standing around are here on serious business. They are here to buy and sell horses, draft horses, and the rest of the world is of little interest to them today.

Everywhere little white sales pamphlets are being folded over; pencil stubs mark an animal of interest, a good price, an old friend's address. Knowing glances are exchanged between neighbours and friendly advice is exchanged by strangers. In the ring a man with a whip lightly touches a Percheron mare on the rump as she is trotted by. She bucks. To the experienced eye this shows good spirit and the bidding goes higher.

# The Royal Agricultural Winter Fair

If the full majesty, beauty and power of the horse can be seen anywhere, surely it is at the Royal Winter Fair in Toronto each year. The fair is really an agricultural event, a farm show; but it is a great farm show and the equestrian events offer one of the best horse shows in the land.

Here you see prime equine bloodstock, the best horsemanship, the balletic precision of dressage, the split-second thrill of jumping, the grace and form of the trotters and the show-harnessed, powerful, draft-horse teams.

# he Milk Horse

ll prefer the horse for delivering. I don't know; there
omething a little more personal, I suppose. It's kind of
icult to explain. Just a feeling, you know. There's another
e to using the horse as well. See, I usually take milk for
ee, four houses at a time. Well, when I've been to the
house I don't have to get back to a truck because Nell,
horse, is already there waiting for me.

ained her myself, you know. It takes a while, a good two
three months. When we first got her she'd never been into
vn. She was a farm horse, you see. Anyway, I couldn't
her over the bridge. Had a heck of a time with her. It
s a bad day as well. I had to lead her across. But after two
nths I never had any trouble with her. She only left me

once, bolted like. She was standing by a railway-siding here
and something scared her. Well, she took right off, straight
into the centre of town before someone stopped her. But
she was alright after.

"Actually, it's harder for her now. When I got her and broke
her in, she learned to stop at every house where I delivered
the milk. Now people have moved off and others come
in and you might miss out ten houses, so she gets mixed up.
But she still knows her route. She's had to learn the new
ones just like me. And it sure has changed around here in

Milkman Don Courneyea of Foster's Dairy in Tweed, Ontario, and his horse, Nell, making their daily delivery.

e last while. Up the end of town there, it's all families
ow. There wasn't a house there fifteen years ago. Now
ere's a whole lot of new people we serve.

's the same old thing everyday, just like any job. It gets a
t dull sometimes. But I've got a lot of friends; I know
retty near everybody, except some of the newer ones. The
wn is changing. People getting old and leaving for the
ties and that.

hen we were going to get rid of the horse and float here,
efore the oil crisis that was, the people, the townsfolk
ound, got really upset about it. That was kind of nice,
ou know.

"But you have to face the way things are. Now with the town getting that much bigger the horse is a bit slow to reach the houses on the outskirts. I reckon this sort of delivery is pretty well on the way out now. I mean, there is no time for horses in the cities, is there? I don't really know if it is perhaps always right. Maybe they'll come back one day. It would be nice, I reckon."

# Fox-hunting

The hunter should be a strong horse with stout legs, good spirit and a patient disposition. It must be able to walk, trot, stand, or gallop all day long over strange and rough fields. It has to be able to jump fences and ditches with grace enough to maintain its rider's position. And at the day's end the hunter must trot gently back home. Dispute the virtues of fox-hunting if you like, but the sight of a hunt in full cry over the fields is pure beauty.

# Racing

"Why do people go to the races? Well, I don't know; but I think that for anybody who can appreciate the horse as a beautiful animal, a day at the races is terrific. Particularly in the good races. The great horses, you know. There is this competitive spirit they have. They're straining with positively everything they have to get by another horse or not let another horse get by. This is really what racing is all about. This is the beauty. Now it doesn't necessarily happen with every race, but that's what you go to see. Then of course there's the excitement, the entertainment side; lots of colour and atmosphere if you like that sort of thing.

"I think that the gambling aspect, the betting, is not a factor to all racing fans. Of course there is that challenge of trying to take the mumbo-jumbo around the track, the facts and figures in the racing form, and reckoning all that, trying to pick a winner. Hoping that you can pick a winner that pays a big price, which means the public is wrong with its favourite. It means that you as an individual handicapper are smarter than all the others. And if you do have a buck on it, well, that can be quite a thrill then.

"You put on forty dollars to win or maybe a couple of hundred; you know that it's risky. That's the lure, isn't it? It all depends on how much you are willing to put on your hunches. Sometimes, no matter what you do, you get losers; and there's nothing you can do about it. But then you get a couple of winners and forget about the lousy time you had last week and play another horse. Most of the winnings don't get too high, of course; you know, twenty, thirty, forty dollars. But they let you keep on going. It's all a part of the excitement.

"Some people go to the races like they go to a football game or that. They bet a few dollars here and there but they're not here really, except to be entertained. Other people spend hours and hours at home reading, studying the racing form and keeping records. When they go to the track to lay a bet, they probably know that horse as well as its owners do. Or they hope they do, because maybe they are going to put a bundle on him. When you're betting big money, you've got to know the horses you're investing in. But I've seen people here with more money than sense, and I've seen them lose it all. And usually they blame the horse. Well, I ask you, is it the horse's fault?

"There are people I know who say they have systems. Some I know bet on colours; they bet a grey horse or a black. Some won't bet on a horse with one white leg. Oh, there are as many systems as there are gamblers. Now I'm not an expert or that, not as compared to some handicappers; but I know good spirit and movement, I think. And it doesn't matter what colour the horse is, if he's coming in first, no matter what colour he is, I'll bet him.

"I've been back to the stables a few times. It's not that easy to get to the stables though. I go mainly through these people I know that have a horse. That is really interesting there,

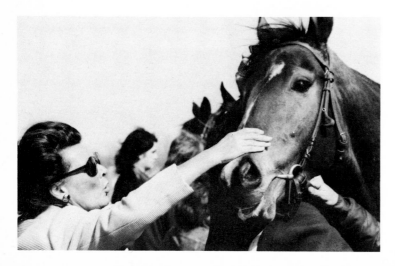
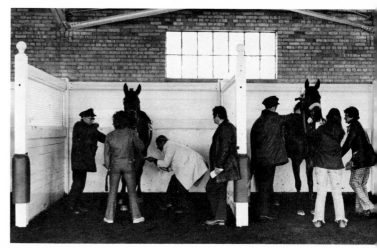

around the stables. The horses you know, you see them just like any other horses. It loses that entertainment aspect. They are just beautiful animals. And, of course, you can talk to the stable people there, the grooms and that, listen to the talk that's going around. Maybe you can get a tip or something.

"If I've got a favourite, a horse that I've followed through the form for a while and maybe want to bet a good bit on him, I try to get a look at him if possible. See how he's being looked after, see the way he's handled and that. If you think he looks a bit off maybe you'll not bet that day. It's all where your interest lays, but I get a lot more interest personally from a race this way.

"Some people I know, they keep telling me to buy my own horse. Oh, I looked into it many times, you know. I don't know though. Actually I had my eye on a yearling a while ago. But no. I think I'll stay away from it. Well, let's put it this way. If I were ever successful enough in an outside venture to throw a lot of money around, then maybe. Well, even then, I don't think I'd bother. Being an owner would take the fun out of it all really.

"There is the paddock. Now a lot of people don't worry that much about going to the paddock; they'd rather stay in the club-house. The paddock is really where you should decide whether to bet a horse or not. Whether to go for place or win or whatever. You see, once you've handicapped a horse – picked him out, looked at the way he's been going

at the other races, followed his form – then you look at him in the paddock to see what he's like among the competition. You see how he's moving, how he's behaving, whether or not he's in a sweat, if he's looking calm or fretted up. You can get a better perspective, you see. Maybe he's got bandages on that could indicate a strain. Maybe he looks fine and you put a big bet on him and if your choice is right, well, that's really the game, isn't it, playing a hunch.

"Now there are many people to whom the paddock means a different thing altogether. To them the paddock is the snob side of racing. Well, I can't take that too much. Look at the Queen's Plate there. Everybody gets into their Sunday best or whatever. It gets so it's like a fashion parade. But if that's what people like, well, it's all right for a couple of days, holidays and that; but it takes away the real feel of racing I think. And the horses, you know, all those frilly dresses the women wear, the horses get scared and fret up. Personally I think it's ridiculous. I mean the Queen's Plate is not exactly my favourite day at the races, but I go of course

"The horses there in a race like the Plate are the cream of the horse world. They're elegant. And in a good race you get to see the real competitive blood. It's a beautiful thing, that is, to see two horses neck and neck for three-quarters of a mile or a mile, you know, nostril to nostril, all the way around for a photo. It's phenomenal. It's something to cheer for, something to participate in. You can't tell someone that feeling, it's something special you've got to experience for yourself."

Opposite. Harness racing on a
snowy night at Toronto's Greenwood
race track. Below. Horses strain at
the start of a race at the
Charlottetown Driving Park in
Prince Edward Island.

# Threshermen's Reunion

Austin in southern Manitoba is a small prairie farming town. It is proud of the agricultural heritage of the Province and looks back with respect and warmth to the days of the horse, the days of the teams of twenty or more horses pulling cumbersome old combines, the days of threshing and haying with a horse and wagon.

Much of this way of life and the machinery that propelled it have been preserved at the Manitoba Agricultural Museum and Homesteaders' Village near Austin. Here hundreds of implements, tools and machines from the days of the draft horse have been gathered together. There are ploughs, harrows, discs, buck-rakes, hay-rakes, mowers. There are also more complex machines like binders, combines, hay-loaders and even an old hay press powered by horses harnessed to a turn-style machine that looks much like a living merry-go-round. Most of the machines donated to the museum since it opened in 1953 are still in working order, and some are used to work the museum's own farm.

The Threshermen's Reunion which takes place each July at the Museum is a great experience. For what can only be described as a four-day-fling, farmers and stockmen from all over the area gather together to relive the ways of the past. All the old machinery and implements are put to work. The spectacles to be seen include saw-mills in operation, ploughing matches, parades, haying and threshing.

The threshing competition held each afternoon is an incredible sight. Teams of farmers with old threshing machines try to out-thresh one another, traction engines belching smoke, horses pulling wagons of sheaves at break-neck speed around the arena. Besides providing good fun, the threshing competition also offers a rare glimpse of what it must have been like when the horse was everywhere, just a generation ago.

A ploughman checks and shapes
the line of his furrows during a
ploughing competition.

# loughing Match

horses hereabouts have almost gone now, I suppose,
m regular working like. Yes, years ago near every farm
l a team or two entered in the match. Fine horses. There
s a pride, in those days, in the way your team turned out.
en just on the farm you tried to make your team look
od. And they knew it as well. They like a little bit of care;
y work a bit better with a little care, I think. That was a lot
lo then, cleaning the harness and that, keeping it supple
e. See, if it got dirty and hard, it would likely dry up
l crack on you.

father – it was all horses in his days, mind – he used to
e a great deal of pride in his ploughing. Yes, he'd be
egular at the matches. He'd practise with the farm plough-
. He had a saying 'Six by nine and straight as a line.' In
competitions and that you would plough a good furrow
inches deep and nine wide. Now that sounds easy to
st fellas, I guess, but it takes a lot on you and your horse.

ere are still a good many matches about now, you know.
t as many as before, but they're getting more popular now
h the city folk. Well, that's good. I like to see the interest
ain. Lots come up and ask questions and that. Well, you
to answer them as much as you like. Try to tell them
at it's like working with the horses. Why we do it and that.
st, you know, they think that it's only at the fairs and
tches like this that the horse ploughing gets done. They
ve around the highways in their cars and all they ever
is tractors working the land. But some of us still like to
the horse, not many now, I reckon, but still enough.
ck, you get kind of sick of all the gas fumes and dirt with
ctors, but working with the horses you get kind of closer,
u know, closer to the earth.

st of the men who are ploughing regular like, they are the
es who enter the matches most, I suppose. Then there are
ew that just have a team as a hobby, more for fun. But
ou really want to compete in a match like this one, with
ms from all over the world, you have to keep working,
ays getting a bit better. You take some of the teams here,
they come out only to win. You can't talk to them or nothing
and if they don't win some really don't like it much. I suppose
I can understand that, but I don't hold with grudges much
myself. Matches like this, well, to me they're more of a time
to meet up with people again. Friends and that. Some you
might not see at all except at the fairs. It's all kind of friendly.

"Me, I think there is more to ploughing with a team than a
tractor. Yes. You know, you have to have a good under-
standing with the horse. With a tractor you turn a few
handles, keep a good line and that's about it. With a team,
if you get one that gets a bit frisky, there's little you can do.
Other times you might just be going along fine; the soil is
good, the grass not too long and maybe you come in with a
prize. I got first and second a few times. Well, that's nice also,
you know. You celebrate a bit then. You give an extra treat
or two to the horses and that.

"A while back, I reckon, most people thought the matches
would end like. You know, with all the interest in everything
modern, the space age and that. But lately, in the last five
years or so, it seems there is more interest in the horse. I guess
that's good, keeping a bit of the old country ways alive.
Heck, we've lost so many of the crafts and skills that it's
good there's still people who remember the old horse."

Two-horse, single-furrow plough
contests, such as the one held at
the International Ploughing Match
near Oshawa, Ontario, are
becoming very popular again. With
the reins tight around his back and
only his voice to command his
team, the ploughman has to control
and balance the plough to cut an
even furrow.

134

# Carriage-maker

The buggy-maker was the automobile-manufacturer of the horse age. Many men made handsome livings building wagons and buggies in those days. The demand was great, especially at the turn of the century when cities were growing rapidly. In rural areas wagons were often built at home with the help of the local blacksmith. A carriage, however, required the services of a specialist, a man who could work the wood, fit the leather, build the springs and make travel along the rough roadways as comfortable as possible. Today, in spite of the interest shown in old wagons pulled by teams of horses at shows and fairs, the craft of buggy- and carriage-making has been all but lost. Fortunately in reclusive communities such as the Mennonite area around Elmira, Ontario, where the working horse is very much a part of the daily life, the carriage-maker can still be seen working at his craft in much the same atmosphere as a hundred years ago.

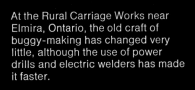

At the Rural Carriage Works near Elmira, Ontario, the old craft of buggy-making has changed very little, although the use of power drills and electric welders has made it faster.

# Mennonites

The Mennonites in the area around Elmira in southern Ontario are proudly religious people with a code of peace and simple living. Mennonites of the old order abhor modern technology and prefer to live in the style of the past. Today the more moderate members of the church gladly make use of most modern conveniences such as electricity and trucks. But horses as working animals are still very much in demand among the Mennonites and perform all the chores they were once essential for.

Opposite. After being cut with a binder, the corn stooks are loaded onto wagons and taken to the threshing machines on land near Elmira, Ontario. Below. On a late fall day farmers and their teams take a break from harrowing to shelter from the rain.

# Alvie Coates, Farmer

lvie Coates is a stocky, jovial farmer in his mid-sixties
ith the speedy sing-song dialect of the Maritimes. His farm
ear Amherst, Nova Scotia is about a hundred and thirty
cres in area. When I arrived on the farm, Alvie was out in
e field with Jip and Jane, his Clydesdale team, digging
e new season's potatoes. After I helped him bag up a few
undredweight of these famous Maritime spuds, we sat and
lked in the mid-day sun.

hasn't changed for me much. In the old days we used to
the ploughing, harrowing and that when I was a kid. That
as with my father's team; they were Percherons. I always
ked Percherons myself pretty well. I've got a Clyde team
w though. I changed over when I needed a new team a
hile ago. I thought they looked good, kindly, you know;
ey make a good team.

ears ago we used to go around with the old hay press,
ound the country. Sometimes we'd be away a couple of
ays pressing hay; it was long distances with a team in the
mmer. We'd have maybe two teams of horses on the press,
d another team hauling the gasoline engine behind. They
ere big horses, really big. I guess they weighed a good ton
ch.

metimes it could be quite a struggle with a team though.
ou've got to be strong with them. There's only one team
at ever got away from me. I was on an old wagon going
r a load of hay down River Hill when the big neck-yoke
roke, the pole dropped down and hit them on the rump.
hey just took off. I was alright though, lucky mind. They
idn't get too far before I caught up with them. But I'm
tting too old for that sort of thing now.

the winter sometimes we used to hay out at what we called
e Bay Marsh. It's a way out on Amherst Point; it's out to
a now. We used to get up at four in the morning, milk
e cows, do the chores, take the team way out there on the
arsh, get a load of hay on and come back. It was really
ld out there, miserable. We used to cut the hay in the
summer and stack it up out there. In the winter we'd go
across fields wherever we could go; the snow was too deep
and the roads were no better than the fields. We just took
the horses wherever they could make a track for themselves.

"You'd share a lot with the horses, you know, good and bad.
You would become sort of friends with each other. Getting
out all day there with them, having your lunch with them
and that. There was no time for moods with them though.
No, they would soon feel it, you know.

"We used to go into Amherst, me and the boys, once a week
with the team. We'd pull into the old blacksmith shop, get
some shoeing done maybe, get the stores and, er, we'd always
get a bottle of something for the way back, to cheer us up
like. Yes, then you didn't mind coming back so much; the
road seemed too short then.

"I like to keep the horses pretty well always in the barn, feed
them in there. It's right near the house. They get hay and
grain with some turnips. Maybe this time of the year I
feed them some carrots or a few potatoes, and a few treats
I give them. They like a bit of candy if they've been good.
They always enjoy it if I find I have a couple of peppermints
around my pocket, you know."

Preceding pages. Alberta farmer
Don Holgerson with his team of
Belgians cutting summer hay with
an old style mower. Below. Don's
older daughter helps unharness the
horses at the day's end.

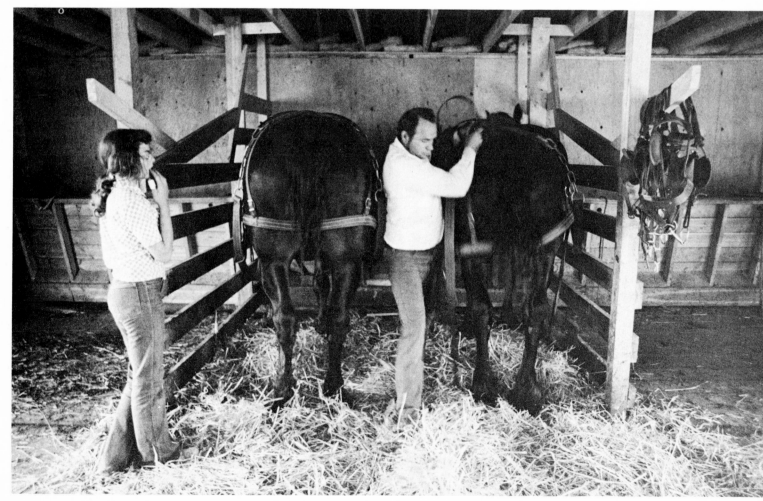

# Don Holgerson of Bonnyville, Alberta

For most of the past decade Don Holgerson, his wife and two children have lived on and successfully worked a good-sized farm in Bonnyville, Alberta. They use no modern power sources such as gas or electricity and rely solely on their horse teams for working the land.

With a small horse farm like ours, the farm is not just an occupation; it's a way of life. It reflects the outlook of a person, his attitudes to living standards and pressures. You can't work it on a clock, in a mechanical way. There have to be opportunities to take things slower and perhaps with more personal involvement.

The working day is different, of course. The amount of work covered is certainly less with a horse than a tractor, but the pride in the workmanship is something that too few, I think, recognize today. You are right there with your implement; you see what's going on. You can make slight adjustments as you go along, which you can't do on a tractor because of the greater acreage being worked. Then you're constantly resting your team and so you have time to observe. You become more aware of what's going on around you and you become a better farmer because of this.

We should really take a close look again at the small farm and everything that went with it. And if the draft horse is to play a big role on the family farm, as it can, as a source of power, where are we going to find people with the know-how to operate them? That's the question. Oh, a lot was published in the past and I daresay some of it will find its way back into publication again. But one of the things we're failing to do in our agricultural schools is teaching young people about the draft horse. We shouldn't assume that they don't want to know. This happens too often. They should really have a choice about using horses or not.

"A lot of young fellows, I'm sure, would just as soon be out on a farm like this one, producing most of their own food and deriving most of their living from this way of life. It's probably frustrating for them because they don't know how to start. It's not like it was in the eighteen hundreds, when you knew free land was available. It's not just a matter of going out and finding your piece and taking up a homestead.

"I suppose it comes down to making a choice. You see, on a farm like this a man spends a lot of time looking after his daily basic requirements. Whereas if he has everything supplied, everything 'modern', these needs are looked after for him. He doesn't have to spend hours making sure there's enough firewood to keep him warm or carrying in drinking water. These things today are rather automatic. But with the type of farming we're talking about, these basic needs have to be met each day.

"Now if we didn't enjoy this, we certainly wouldn't do it. I mean, there's no law that says we have to live this way. But we enjoy farming this way with the horses and we produce enough to feed ourselves and, well, quite a few other people besides. We enjoy, I guess, the feeling of independence or self-sufficiency we get in this type of life. And it isn't all hard work and no play by any means. We have picnics and hayrides and the neighbours come over. Like I said, it's a good life; we don't have any complaints. I think we have just as much free time as anyone else; it's just that we spend it differently.

Seven-year-old Crissie Holgerson rides her favourite horse towards home. As horses are the only power used on the farm, they have become very much a part of the family's life.

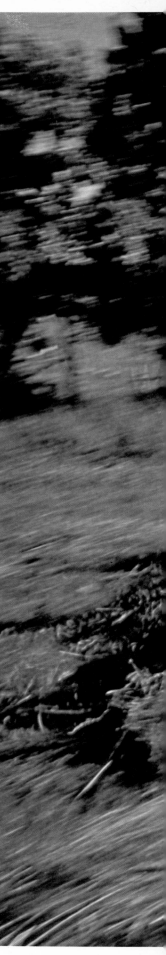

"Basically there's only so many dollars you can get out of a small farm like this, even with the best management. And if you're going to spend that money on mechanization and lots of off-farm services, then it becomes really difficult to make a small farm work. In other words, if you have a gross income between seven and eight thousand dollars, like we do, and your operating expenses don't exceed two thousand dollars or so; then you have a net income, a real income, of five thousand dollars. But if you're running a 'modern' farm and paying out a large part of the income on tractor payments, loans and off-farm services, then you just can't do it. You just never make a profit. You get caught up in buying more land to pay for more machinery, and then you have to buy more machinery to work the land. You can get caught in that spiral and then just can't get out of it.

"Let me tell you about our harvest a couple of years ago; it was in the fall of '73. It was such a wet, nasty fall that the grain wouldn't dry and just laid there in the swath. Of course, with a horse farm like ours, we cut with a binder and the grain stands up to a stook and dries easier. Anyway, it was really wet and the big farms couldn't get their tractors onto the land and their crops got snowed under. But since our grain was standing up in the stooks, we were able to get it all threshed there before the snows came. We had about a hundred inches of snow that time and most in the area lost their crops. The big mechanical farms looked at us with a little envy, I think. Not only did we get our grain off but we were able to get all our fall ploughing done as well, because we were able to keep going in the wet with the horses without them getting stuck in the mud and digging up the soil like tractors.

"This is where it's difficult to justify the mechanized units. The only way they can really take over is by tearing down the older system, with horses, like ours. It wasn't that the older way didn't work. It did. We have hundreds of years to prove that. The people who deny that are just repeating what they've been told over and over again by the – and this is unfortunate – by the high-pressure agro-business people.

I mean, farmers are their customers and they don't want them to say all of a sudden, 'Well, gee, I don't think I'll buy that tractor' or 'I don't need as much fuel this year because I'm going over to horse power.' Or that they won't want chemical fertilizers because they are going to use the crop-rotation system from now on. No, the sales people don't like to hear this kind of thing at all.

"But I think we will see the horse back in use more and more, mainly because of the energy costs which are going to increase continually in the next decade or so. People are going to find it economical to use the horse for many jobs that they use tractors for at the moment. Winter choring is a good example, and some of the lighter tillage jobs. Obviously the big super-market type spreads will need tractors and every piece of machinery for their work, but they will be so expensive to run that the average farm won't be able to afford it. It's happening to a small extent already. We breed horses here, you know, and now we are getting a lot of interest from the big boys, especially on the stock farms where they can use teams for feeding the stock in the winter. I mean, horses are quicker in snow than a truck or tractor.

"Horses may come back into urban areas as well. There's no reason why horses can't transport goods around towns as well as trucks. It all depends how far our leaders want to see; how smart, how concerned they really are. We can't go on forever the way we are and we're going to have to make big adjustments. Maybe we should start making small ones now. Then we could gradually learn to live a different kind of life, with the horse as a very useful power source. It's not a new way, but we can't go on as we are at the moment. Surely it's better to return gradually, starting now, than to wait ten or fifteen years and then have the gas and luxuries we're used to taken away all at once. That would be a catastrophe, a true culture shock."

These photographs were taken over a three-year period.
At the time of writing, at least one of the subjects in the book
had died and several of the horses were no longer being worked.
Perhaps we should take a look at what is left and try to preserve it.